GEORGIAN LIFE

BY

JOHN GUY

COUNTRY LIFE

CROP ROTATION

A new system of crop rotation was introduced whereby, instead of leaving one field fallow each year, a different crop was grown over a four year period to keep the soil fertile.

*T*he open landscape of the middle ages changed dramatically during the Georgian period. Between 1750–1850 over 2,500 Enclosure Acts were passed giving landowners the right to fence in their fields. Much of the common and rented land was lost to villagers as a result and many were forced to find work in factories in the towns. Faced with eviction and starvation, many people rioted against the changes.

MAN POWER

This hoist, known as a 'rat's tail crane' (of c.1752) would have been a familiar sight at quarries, brickfields, foundries and mines. It was operated by men or horses walking inside the wheel.

BIRTHPLACE OF THE INDUSTRIAL REVOLUTION

The first industrial factories were set in rural locations close to rivers, like these iron foundries in Coalbrookdale, Shropshire, where Abraham Darby constructed the first iron bridge in the world. It is still to be seen in the nearby town of Ironbridge.

AGRICULTURAL REVOLUTION

The new advances in industrial technology meant more and more people left the countryside to work in factories in the towns. Many new machines were invented to increase the productivity of the land to feed the burgeoning population, such as this seed drill, designed by Jethro Tull to ensure a more efficient method of sowing seeds.

ROOM WITH A VIEW

The rich lived in large country estates to escape the filth of industrial towns. When Mereworth Castle (Kent) was built in 1723, the original village was moved half-a-mile down the road to improve the view from the house.

LIFE IN TOWNS

Like many others who formerly worked on the land but were forced to try and make a living in the towns, this street pedlar wandered the streets selling his wares. Amongst the items for sale are brushes, medicines and, in his hand, spectacles.

O f the many changes that occurred at this time, the growth of towns is perhaps the most significant. New technology in both farming and industry signalled the move for most people away from the country to the towns, marking the beginning of modern urbanisation. Towns could not cope with this sudden influx; poor sanitary conditions and the lack of clean drinking water caused frequent outbreaks of disease.

HUSTLE AND BUSTLE

This engraving by Hogarth gives a good idea of the noise, chaos and crowds that were a common feature of Georgian towns.

UNPLANNED TOWNS

Towns grew in an unplanned, piecemeal fashion, with prestigious new developments often placed alongside slums in filthy streets. Many towns still had unsurfaced roads, which were impassable in wet weather.

STREET LIGHTING

From about 1730 experiments had been made with using various gases as a source of light, but it was not until gas was successfully extracted from coal after about 1801 that lighting on a large scale became possible. This picture shows the euphoria that was often generated when towns installed gas street lighting.

FACELIFT

Many town centres received a facelift or were completely rebuilt in the Georgian period in classical style. This view of Westminster Bridge was painted by Canaletto.

LIFE FOR THE RICH

SPOILED CHILDREN

Life for rich children was often privileged, shielded from the harsh realities of the drudgery experienced by poor children.

*N*ever before had there been such a gulf between the rich and poor. The shift in wealth, and power, away from the landed gentry to the new entrepreneurs of industry, created many social problems. The fortunes amassed by the rich were at the direct expense of the poor, who were ruthlessly exploited. The divisions in society between the 'haves' and the 'have-nots' eventually led to open revolt, forcing Parliament to pass several reform bills.

DINNER PARTIES

Georgians liked to entertain at home, especially in small informal groups. After dinner, the guests would entertain one another by playing musical instruments or singing.

DEDICATED FOLLOWERS OF FASHION

'Dandies' were fashion-conscious people who took their appearance rather too seriously, almost to the point of obsession.

SOCIAL ORDER

Although there has always been a class system
in Britain, the Georgian period exaggerated
the divisions between the social hierarchy.
The wealth generated by industry
created several new tiers of middle-
class businessmen.

FINE CRAFTSMANSHIP

This delightful pocket watch, made about
1759, with its silver pair-case, is a good
example of the fine craftsmanship of the
period, which would not have been possible
without patronage from the rich.

THE POOR AT HOME

In the early years of the industrial revolution many people who formerly worked on the land secured jobs in the growing textile industry. Initially, much of the work could be done at home by 'outworkers'. The whole family helped, but as technology improved most people were forced to work in the factories.

SOCIAL REFORMER

Anthony Ashley Cooper, 7th Earl of Shaftesbury (1801-85), championed the cause of the poor and spent most of his life fighting in Parliament for social reforms. He was responsible for helping the homeless, improving working conditions and reducing working hours in factories and mines, especially for women and children.

ONE-ROOMED HOVELS

Houses for the poor remained cramped and unhealthy. Sometimes a whole family had to live in one or two roomed cottages, with no drainage or running water and little heating.

LACK OF PRIVACY

Flushing toilets were an expensive rarity in Georgian times. The poor had to use outside, communal toilets. Indoors, they used chamber pots which were emptied into open drains when full.

WORKING UNDER GROUND

As the momentum of the industrial revolution grew, so did the demand for coal. Mines were inhospitable and dangerous places. Because of the confined spaces, women and children did much of the work, spending up to 14 hours a day underground.

THE TOLPUDDLE MARTYRS

In 1834 six villagers from Tolpuddle, Dorset, were arrested for joining a trade union, which was illegal. The marchers shown here presented a petition to William IV, but to no avail. The villagers were sentenced to seven years hard labour in Australia.

FOOD & DRINK

The growth of Britain's empire opened up new trade routes abroad. Many new foodstuffs were imported, especially from the colonies, such as potatoes, tomatoes and sugar. Britain became one of the best fed countries in Europe, certainly for the rich, although even the lower classes ate better than their counterparts on the Continent.

EXOTIC PLANTS

Many new foods were brought back to England from around the world, such as the aubergine and the Artocarpus, or bread fruit. Others, like the Myrmecodia Beccarii from Australia, shown here, were collected by Captain Cook on his various expiditions for botanical study at Kew Gardens.

A FINE VINTAGE

A greater variety of drinks became available during the Georgian era. Wine, of course, has been popular since Roman times, but increased travel made more vintages available from other countries. Tea and coffee houses became fashionable places to meet and exchange news.

CHANGING HABITS

As the population moved from the country to towns, many could no longer produce their own food, which they bought instead from the growing number of shops.

DENTAL HYGIENE

Very little dental treatment was available, usually consisting only of the removal of bad teeth - without anaesthetic. Dental powders were used to keep teeth clean, while tongue scrapers might help to keep the palate fresh.

AFTERNOON TEA

Tea was first introduced to Britain about 1650. By the late 18th century tea-drinking had become a popular social habit among all classes, but particularly the rich. This ornate tea-caddy is typical of the period.

SELECTIVE BREEDING

Whereas previously most livestock was slaughtered at the start of winter and the meat stored, improved harvests meant that animals could now be overwintered and fed root crops. Special breeds, like this short-horned bull, were also developed to create large, more productive livestock.

PASTIMES

The Georgian period was an era of great elegance and contrasts, devoted to the pursuance of pleasure, at least for the rich. While the poor struggled for survival, enjoying simple pleasures in the few hours break from work they had, like dancing, going to fairs or cock-fighting, the rich enjoyed themselves to the point of extravagance, gambling, hunting and attending an endless round of balls and dinners.

A DIFFERENT BEAT

With the increased interest in music and dancing, the manufacture of musical instruments received an added impetus in Georgian times. This unusual square drum dates from the 1830s.

TAKE YOUR PARTNERS

Music and dance featured strongly in Georgian society. New, risqué dances were introduced from Europe, such as the waltz, which was thought immodest and caused a sensation.

PLEASURE GARDENS

Landscaped parks and gardens were laid out in fashionable parts of towns, where people could promenade or attend concerts. These silver admission tokens are to Vauxhall Gardens, London.

CRUEL SPORT

Cock fighting was a cruel blood sport, popular since the Middle Ages. Cockerels, fitted with metal spurs, fought to the death, while onlookers bet on the outcome.

ON GUARD

As the methods of warfare changed with the increased use of firearms, the art of swordplay, or fencing, came to be regarded more as an upper class sport.

MUSICAL EVENINGS

One of the most popular pastimes amongst the wealthy was after-dinner musical evenings. Each guest was expected to contribute to the entertainment by playing a musical piece or singing.

CURTAIN UP

Theatre-going was popular among all classes, particularly with the growth of theatres in the provinces, like this one at Scarborough. Playwrights such as Sheridan were popular, as were musical revues, comedies and bawdy romps.

FASHION

The new technology in the textile industry revolutionised clothes design. The manufacture on a large scale of new materials like cotton, coupled with the import of exotic materials such as silk, made more elaborate designs possible. The Georgians had a fairly liberal attitude towards sex, which was reflected in their clothes design. In the mid-1780s fashionable dresses had grotesquely enlarged busts and bustles, using frames and padding. By the 1790s see-through tops on dresses were the dominant style in high society.

SOBER TASTE

This picture of a 'dandy' shows the exaggerated wig hairstyles often sported by fashionable men of the day. The most notable figure of the period, perhaps, was George 'Beau' Brummel, who dressed with exquisite, yet sober taste in preference to showy display.

MASQUERADE

The upper classes were quite promiscuous and masquerade balls gave them the perfect opportunity for flirting. Another very fashionable pursuit of the rich was to visit asylums and watch the antics of the unfortunate inmates.

UNDERSTATED

A typical family group in late Georgian times, when the excesses of earlier years had become slightly more understated.

PERSONAL HYGIENE

Both men and women were quite fastidious about their personal hygiene and liked to wear scents based on concentrated floral and herbal extracts. This delightful perfume box, containing 12 different scents, is shaped to resemble a book when closed.

ELEGANT STYLES

This dress of brocaded silk, of 1747, is typical of the elegant styles produced. The bustle at the back was achieved by draping the material over a wooden or metal framework.

ART & ARCHITECTURE

*L*ike so much else in the Georgian era, art and architecture underwent great periods of change. Revolutionary new ideas swept the country, especially among the poets of the age, like Keats, Byron, Coleridge and Wordsworth. Daniel Defoe's 'Robinson Crusoe' was published, probably the first 'great' English novel. The Prince Regent was a great patron of the arts responsible for the royal collection of paintings and the National Gallery. Artists, like Constable and Gainsborough, created new fashions in nature paintings.

AN ARTIST'S PALETTE

18th and 19th century artists often mixed their own paints from chemical compounds or plant extracts, such as this smalt, a blue pigment of unknown origin, making it difficult to repeat shades exactly. Many of the compounds they used were poisonous.

INSPIRED GENIUS

The Georgian period saw many changes in the field of art, when old ways were cast off in favour of new ideas. The revolutionary impressionistic technique developed by Turner inspired generations of later artists. In his lifetime he produced an incredible 25,000 paintings, etchings and drawings. The picture shown here is 'Rain, Steam and Speed', reflecting the spirit of the age.

ORIENTAL PALACE

The Prince Regent (later George IV) commissioned John Nash to redesign his house at Brighton (where he stayed when taking his regular sea-water health cures) into a palace. Nash skillfully unified the Prince's fascination with oriental and Indian art into the extravaganza of Brighton Pavilion.

INSPIRED BY ROME

Georgian architects looked to the classical building styles of ancient Rome for their inspiration. Many town centres, including London, were rebuilt at this time, but few towns can rival the elegance and unity of design of Bath, with its beautiful crescents and terraces.

GOTHIC HORROR

One of the masterpieces of popular horror fiction was conceived at this time, 'Frankenstein'. It was written by Mary Shelley, second wife of the romantic poet Percy Bysshe Shelley and was conceived one rainy afternoon when she, Shelley and Lord Byron, whilst staying in Switzerland, had a competition amongst themselves to see who could write the most frightening horror story.

HEALTH & MEDICINE

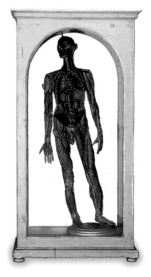

HOW THE BODY WORKS

This anatomical model, dating from 1776–80, shows the venous and blood-flow system within the body. It was made of wax and used for teaching purposes in hospitals.

*I*mportant new discoveries were made into the causes of disease and in understanding the anatomy of the human body. Much of the research was carried out by doctors using corpses supplied by grave robbers or execution victims. The major health problems came from poor sanitation in overcrowded towns, with frequent outbreaks of diseases such as typhoid and cholera.

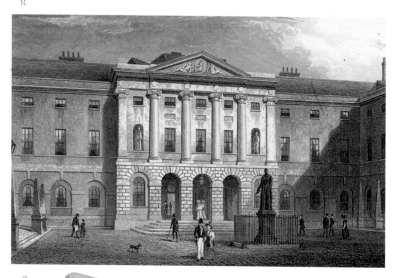

GUY'S HOSPITAL

Guy's Hospital, London, was founded in 1722 by Thomas Guy, with proceeds from selling his shares in the South Sea Company before the bubble burst. Always at the forefront of advancing medical knowledge, it remains one of the finest teaching hospitals in the world.

SURGICAL IMPLEMENTS

This piston-action syringe is made of ivory and was probably used to syphon off blood or extract poisons.

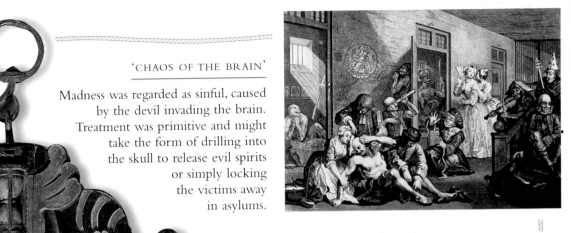

'CHAOS OF THE BRAIN'

Madness was regarded as sinful, caused by the devil invading the brain. Treatment was primitive and might take the form of drilling into the skull to release evil spirits or simply locking the victims away in asylums.

DRASTIC MEASURES

This case of surgical instruments from the 18th century resembles a carpenter's tool box and contains implements used to carry out amputations, a common remedy when little was known about bacterial infections. Over half of all surgical patients died from shock or gangrene.

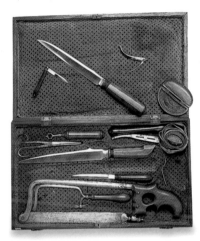

BARBER SURGEONS

Surgery was quite crude and performed without anaesthetics or antiseptics. Operations such as amputations and pulling teeth were usually carried out by barber-surgeons, who combined the unlikely trades of haircutting and surgery, and displayed a sign (an example above) or a red and white striped pole outside their premises.

LADY OF THE LAMP

Although Florence Nightingale is mostly remembered for her work in the Crimean War (1854-56) she was born during the Georgian period (1820). In later life she formed a training school for nurses in St. Thomas's Hospital, London.

LOVE & MARRIAGE

SEARCHING FOR LOVE

Young ladies looking for prospective husbands frequented fashionable venues. This girl is being carried to the waters at Bath in a Sedan chair.

Georgians displayed a fairly liberal attitude towards sex. The age of consent was 14 for boys and 12 for girls. While most people did not marry until their early twenties, teenagers were often quite promiscuous. Rather than face the consequences of having an illegitimate baby, many girls concealed their pregnancies and abandoned or murdered their babies at birth. There was also a high incidence of venereal disease, usually treated by ingesting mercury, which is poisonous.

PRE-NUPTIAL PREGNANCY

Single girls who fell pregnant were encouraged to marry the father of their child, otherwise they might lose their job and be sent to a house of correction.

PARTING OF THE WAYS

Divorced couples could legally separate, but they were forbidden to remarry, except by special Act of Parliament, which was expensive. A common, but illegal, practice amongst the poor was for a man to simply take his spouse to a 'wife-sale' and sell her.

LEGALLY BINDING

Up to 1753 it was possible for any clergyman, no matter how lapsed and unscrupulous he might be, to marry a couple anywhere, frequently for money. After that time, only church weddings were legal.

AFFAIRS OF THE HEART

Nelson had a passionate affair with Lady Emma Hamilton, wife of his friend Sir William Hamilton. She grew obese in later years, as illustrated in this cartoon, where she laments Nelson's departure.

FORBIDDEN FRUITS

As heir to the throne, George IV was forbidden to marry a Catholic, but he married his Catholic mistress, Maria Fitzherbert, in secret in 1785, though the marriage was never officially recognised.

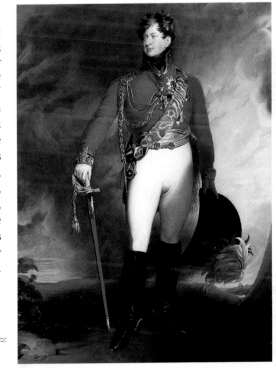

WOMEN & CHILDREN

*M*ost working class women and children worked 12-14 hours a day, six days a week. There were no state-run schools providing free education so only the wealthy could afford to send their children to school. Some textile mill owners provided meals, accommodation and schooling (for boys only) for their child workers.

EDUCATIONAL TOYS

Only the rich could afford this educational magnetic toy, dating from about 1765. Poor children usually played in the street.

A BOOK BEFORE BEDTIME

Educated children from well-off families, who had learned to read and write, could amuse themselves by reading children's books, which began to appear in profusion at this time.

WILL WANDER's WALK,
With both his Companions
And all of their Talk.

Says Will to his Sister
My Dog here proposes,
To take a nice Walk
And just follow our noses.

CHATTELS

In Georgian families all women and children, from all classes, were considered the property of the husband. Any money they earned was his and he was legally allowed to beat or imprison them in the family home.

LOWER WAGES

Factory owners preferred to employ women and children for all but the heaviest jobs because they were paid much lower wages than men for the same work. The noise from the machines was so loud workers had to lip-read in order to communicate.

DANGEROUS WORK

Children were employed to do many of the most dangerous jobs in factories. They had to crawl under the machines (such as this water-powered spinning machine) to clean them or re-tie broken threads, often while the machines were still running. Accident and death rates in factories were high.

LIFE OF LEISURE

By contrast, women from upper class families were not expected to work. Even the housework was done by an army of domestic servants.

WAR AND WEAPONRY

*T*he French leader, Napoleon Bonaparte, tried to build an empire in Europe and threatened to invade Britain. He was eventually defeated by the combined forces of Britain, Prussia, Holland and Belgium, after nearly 22 years of war with France. Britain lost its American colonies in 1781 after an eight year struggle for independence by the colonists.

NAVAL HERO

Vice Admiral Horatio, Lord Nelson, was born in 1758. He went to sea at the age of 12 and rapidly rose to the rank of captain at only 21. He died on board his flagship 'The Victory' at the Battle of Trafalgar in 1805.

ON THE COUNT OF THREE

Firearms improved radically during this period and became much more efficient. The pistol shown here dates from 1789 and is believed to have been used in a duel between the Duke of York and Captain Lennox.

THE BATTLE OF WATERLOO

The Battle of Waterloo took place in a Belgian field on 18th June 1815, where the allied forces under the command of the Duke of Wellington defeated Napoleon's army. At the end of the battle over 60,000 soldiers lay dead, two-thirds of them French.

FIREPOWER

Fighting ships were divided into six different 'rates', according to their size and the number of their guns and crews. A first rate ship was the most powerful, carrying over 100 guns and 800 officers and men. They were expensive to build (about £60,000 – £50 million in today's currency) and might use the wood from 2,000 oak trees.

CRIME & PUNISHMENT

EARLY POLICE FORCE

In 1750 a police office was opened in Bow Street by London magistrate Henry Fielding. The officers were known as 'Bow Street Runners'.

*S*ocial unrest had reached such serious proportions by the 1820s that only radical reforms would stave off outright revolution, as had already been experienced in France. Sir Robert Peel introduced the first organised civilian police force in 1829. In 1832 the Great Reform Bill shifted power away from the landed aristocracy and attempted to reform the voting system.

KEEPING WATCH

From medieval times watchmen, sometimes known as 'charleys', were employed in towns to patrol the streets at night with a staff and lantern and apprehend any wrong-doers.

DARTMOOR PRISON

Punishment was harsh and conditions inside prisons were primitive and open to corruption. Nearly 200 different crimes carried the death sentence, including poaching and picking pockets. Children often received the same punishments as adults, including hanging. Many new prisons were built at this time, including Dartmoor Prison, in Devon, shown above.

HUMAN RIGHTS

The slave trade was seen by William Wilberforce, and other reformers, as a crime against humanity. Slavery was finally abolished throughout the Empire in 1833, after much campaigning.

HIGHWAY ROBBERY

While many people turned to crime as a last resort because of unemployment, others thought it a more lucrative way of life than working for a living. Gangs of robbers terrorised travellers on the highways, frequently resorting to rape, armed assault and murder.

TRANSPORT & SCIENCE

Roads in early Georgian times were in a terrible condition. A system of toll roads was introduced, known as turnpikes, which provided money for improvements. By 1837 there were over 20,500 miles (33,000 kilometres) of turnpikes. The problem of transporting raw materials and finished goods to and from the new factories was overcome by James Brindley, who built several canals linking Britain's towns and rivers with seaports.

THE AGE OF CANALS

The first canal in Britain opened in 1765. By 1815 a network of over 3,700 miles (6000 kilometres) of canals existed, but just 30 years later they were virtually redundant, superseded by the railways.

COMING UP FOR AIR

Halley's diving bell (c.1750) used barrels of fresh air, piped into the chamber. It had a lens on the top for added light and a stop-cock to let out stale air. It was used to salvage wrecks and their valuable cargoes.

THE FIRST MANNED FLIGHT

Several of the pioneers in hot-air ballooning came from France. The Montgolfier brothers made the first public flight using a model balloon in 1783, followed by another a few months later carrying a duck, a sheep and a cockerel. A few weeks after that Pilâtre de Rozier made the first human flight in a balloon over Paris.

BRIGHT SPARKS

Although electricity had been discovered some years before, it was the pioneering work of Humphrey Davy and Michael Faraday that led to the development of modern electric motors. The electrometer shown here dates from 1770.

NEW DESIGNS

Isambard Kingdom Brunel (1806-59), the son of a refugee from the French Revolution, was a brilliant and innovative engineer, specialising in the use of iron and steel in his designs for ships and civil engineering projects.

RAINHILL TRIALS

The directors of the Liverpool-Manchester Railway organised trials to find the best locomotive for their new line. George Stevenson's engine, 'The Rocket', won the competition, marking the beginning of the railway age.

RELIGION

Many people became disillusioned with the complacent attitude displayed by the church and its apparent lack of concern for the social welfare of the poor. While many turned away from the church altogether, others followed the numerous break-away, non-conformist movements that began to appear about this time, including the Methodists, Evangelists and Presbyterians. Church attendance fell off dramatically, particularly among the poor, who worked long hours in the factories and had little time off.

METHODISM

John Wesley (1703-1791) was the 15th of 19 children. He joined a new non-conformist religious group (formed by his brother Charles in 1738) known as the Methodists because of their strict religious observance. He frequently preached in the open air and attracted huge audiences of 20,000 or more.

DEMONIC VISIONS

William Blake (1757-1827) was an artist and poet of rare genius, who claimed to be inspired by visions from God. He had little time for the apathy of the church and regarded the industrial revolution with contempt, its 'dark satanic mills' destroying England's pleasant countryside and creating appalling living conditions.

HELL

MORNING WORSHIP

Most church-goers came from the middle and upper classes, who also observed many religious practices, such as morning and evening prayer, in their own homes.

TRADING PLACES

Slavery was one of the great social evils of
the Georgian period, but the
church did little to alleviate
the suffering. This picture
shows the inhumane
conditions aboard a
slave ship en
route to
America
from Africa.

FALLING
STANDARDS

The title of this
engraving by William
Hogarth is 'The Sleeping
Congregation'. It is a
satirical study
showing just how
low standards had
fallen. Many church reformers blamed the
fall in religious morality on the social
problems brought about by
the industrial revolution.

A GLOSSARY OF INTERESTING TERMS

Bobby - Slang name for a policeman, named after Sir Robert (Bobby) Peel, who set up the first organised police force in 1829.

Militia - A part-time army comprised of local people to supplement the regular army and called out in emergency, usually to quell riots or other civil unrest.

Shuttle - A wooden implement that carries the weft (horizontal threads) back and forth through the warp (vertical threads) on a weaving loom. The word is now applied to anything that goes to and fro repeatedly.

Silly Billy - A term used originally to describe William IV's inept but enthusiastic attempts at government and now used to describe any foolish or incompetent person.

Turn a Blind Eye - The act of of turning a blind eye when we pretend not to see something dates from Nelson's time, when he is said to have deliberately put his telescope to his blind eye in battle so as not to see the signal to withdraw.

United Kingdom - A term used in the Act of Union between Britain and Ireland in 1801 to describe the union of England, Scotland, Wales and Northern Ireland.

Waterloo - The battle in 1815 where Napoleon met his final defeat. The word has since been applied to anyone who gets his come-uppance and receives justice as a result of their actions, i.e. to meet one's Waterloo.

Workhouse - A kind of hostel for the homeless, introduced in 1834, where the poor received food and lodging in return for a day's work.

ACKNOWLEDGEMENTS

We would like to thank: Graham Rich, Tracey Pennington, Liz Rowe and Peter Done for their assistance.

Copyright © 1997 ticktock Publishing Ltd.

First published in Great Britain by ticktock Publishing Ltd., Great Britain. All rights reserved.

No part of this publication may be reproduced, stored in a retrieval system, or transmitted in any form or by any means, electronic, mechanical, photocopying, recording or otherwise, without prior written permission of the copyright owner.

Acknowledgements: Picture Credits t=top, b=bottom, c=centre, l=left, r=right, OFC=outside front cover, IFC=inside front cover, IBC= inside back cover, OBC= outside front cover.

Jonathan Berg/BPL; 28cl. Bodleian Library, University of Oxford: John Johnson Collection; Fashion; 7t, 15t & OFC. Broadlands Trust, Hants./Bridgeman Art Library, London; IFC/1. Spink & Son Ltd., London/Bridgeman Art Library, London; 5br. Roy Miles Gallery, 29 Bruton Street, London W1/ Bridgeman Art Library, London; 13cr. Victoria & Albert Museum, London/ Bridgeman Art Library, London; 15br. Collection of Earl Spencer, Althorp, Northants/Bridgeman Art Library, London; 22bl. © British Museum; 4/5c, 13ct, 31b. Mary Evans Picture Library; 3tl, 8l & OBC, 9t, 13b, 18bl, 19cb, 26tl & OFC, 26bl, 27ct, 29c. E. T. Archive; 9b, 11br. By courtesy of Fine Art Photographic Library; 20/21c, 25c & OFCc. Burlington Paintings/Fine Art Photographic Library; 4bl. Gavin Graham Gallery/Fine Art Photographic Library; 11tl. Mr & Mrs R. Holmes/Fine Art Photographic Library; 30b. Private Collection/Fine Art Photographic Library; 6cr, 11tr. John Mitchell & Son/Fine Art Photographic Library; 23br. Waterhouse & Dodd/Fine Art Photographic Library; 3tr. The Metropolitan Museum of Art, The Elisha Whittelsey Collection, The Elisha Whittelsey Fund, 1959. (59.533.1100). All rights reserved, The Metropolitan Museum of Art; 6tl, 20bl. Museum of London; 4cl, 6b, 9cl, 11bl, 11c, 11cr, 12b, 12/13t, 14l & 32, 14/15b, 20tl, 21t, 25t, 30tl. Reproduced by courtesy of the Trustees, The National Gallery, London; 16/17b. By courtesy of the National Portrait Gallery, London; 21br. National Maritime Museum, London; 19tr, 21cr, 24cl & OFC, 24/25b & OBC, 27tr & OFC, 31tr. Board of Trustees of the National Museums and Galleries on Merseyside (Walker Art Gallery, Liverpool); 9cr. National Trust Photographic Library/Upton House (Bearsted Collection)/Angelo Hornak; 2tl. The Pierpoint Morgan Library, NY. The Elisabeth Ball Collection, PML 84077/Art Resource, NY. The Pierpoint Morgan Library, New York, New York, USA; 22br. Royal Pavilion, Art Gallery and Museums, Brighton; 17tl. The Natural History Museum, London; 10l & OBC. National Railway Museum/Science & Society Picture Library; OFCbr, 29br. Science Museum/Science & Society Picture Library; 2bl & OBC, 3b, 5tr, 7b & OBC, 12tl, 15c, 16cl & OBC, 18tl, 18/19b & OFC, 18/19t, 19cr, 22tl, 23t, 23bl & OBC, 28cb, 28/29c & OFC, 29tr. David Sellman; 16cr. Tate Gallery, London; 30/31t. Universal (Courtesy Kobal); 17r & OBC.

Every effort has been made to trace the copyright holders and we apologise in advance for any unintentional omissions. We would be pleased to insert the appropriate acknowledgement in any subsequent edition of this publication.

A CIP Catalogue for this book is available from the British Library. ISBN 1 86007 004 3